Copyright © 2025 Natoya Cole Evans

All rights reserved.

No part of this publication may be reproduced, distributed, or transmitted in any form or by any means, including photocopying, recording, or other electronic or mechanical methods, without the prior written permission of the publisher, except in the case of brief quotations embodied in reviews and certain other non-commercial uses permitted by copyright law.

DEDICATION

This book is dedicated to the families navigating life across two homes—those learning, day by day, how to move through transitions with patience, understanding, and grace. To the parents, caregivers, and co-parents doing their best in moments that feel uncertain or emotionally heavy, may you be reminded that love can remain steady even when circumstances change. May each handoff, conversation, and new routine be met with compassion, clarity, and a shared commitment to the well-being of the child at the center.

This dedication is also for the children learning that feelings—especially the big, stormy ones—are a natural and important part of growing. For the moments when emotions feel overwhelming, confusing, or hard to name, may this book gently remind you that you are never alone. Your feelings matter. They are signals, not mistakes, and with care, attention, and support, they can always be soothed and understood.

May this book serve as a safe place where emotions are welcomed, curiosity is encouraged, and healing begins. A place where children learn that even when life changes, love remains constant; even when feelings rise like waves, there are tools to help them find calm again. And above all, may every family who opens these pages feel seen, supported, and hopeful—knowing that growth, connection, and peace are always possible.

Winston woke up feeling jittery. Today was his Monday morning at Mom's house, and he wasn't sure he wanted to leave his cozy bed. His blankets felt warm and safe, but school and the week ahead waited for him. He hugged his favorite stuffed animal tightly, wishing he could stay in his soft, calm bubble a little longer.

Even though he loved both homes, moving from one to the other made his tummy twist into knots. He loved playing with toys at Dad's house, and baking cookies at Mom's, but changing homes so quickly sometimes felt overwhelming. "I just don't want to feel nervous all the time," he whispered, wishing someone could make the worry disappear.

At school, the morning rush felt extra hard. The hallway was noisy, backpacks bumping into each other, and everyone seemed to know exactly where they were going. Winston wanted to play and see his friends, but his thoughts were spinning about switching homes later and all the homework and activities waiting for him.

Ms. Lee noticed Winston fidgeting at his desk. She knelt beside him and whispered gently, "Winston, do you want to take a deep breath with me?" Winston hesitated, unsure if it would help, but her kind eyes made him feel safe enough to try.

Winston inhaled slowly… and then exhaled… slowly. He felt a tiny bit calmer, a little less like his tummy was twisting into knots. "It feels… a little better," he whispered. Ms. Lee smiled, reminding him that even small steps could help big feelings feel smaller.

Later, during art time, Winston started drawing the two houses in his head. One had his favorite chair, the other had his favorite blanket. Each house made him happy, but moving between them felt heavy, like carrying two backpacks at the same time. He wished there was a magic bridge to help him switch homes more easily.

At recess, Winston wanted to play tag like the other kids. His mind was spinning with worries about which home he would go to that evening, what homework he might forget, and if he'd have enough time to finish it. The playground felt loud, and he felt small and a little lost.

Ms. Rivera, the school counselor, invited Winston to the calm corner. "Let's name your feelings," she said with a warm smile. Winston wasn't sure how to explain the jumble inside him, but he trusted Ms. Rivera and followed her to the quiet space.

Winston whispered, "I feel… worried and tired." He explained that sometimes his stomach hurt, or his heart felt too fast when it was time to switch homes or go to school. Ms. Rivera nodded, letting him know that his feelings were real and okay to share.

"It's okay," said Ms. Rivera. "Big feelings can come when life changes a lot. We can find ways to calm them, little by little." Winston felt a small flicker of hope. Maybe he could feel better if he learned new ways to handle the storm of feelings inside him.

Winston practiced squeezing a stress ball, drawing his feelings, and breathing slowly. Each little step helped him feel stronger and a bit more in control. He realized he could carry tools inside his backpack that weren't toy tools for his heart and mind.

He talked about Mom's house. "I love being there, but leaving it makes me sad," he said. He felt proud to say it aloud, realizing that sharing feelings made them a little lighter.

"And Dad's house?" asked Ms. Rivera. Winston nodded. "I like it too, but switching homes all the time is confusing. Sometimes it feels like my brain has too many doors open at once." Ms. Rivera nodded, telling him it was normal to feel that way.

Ms. Rivera and Ms. Lee helped Winston make a feelings chart. Red meant anxious, yellow meant worried, and green meant calm. Winston loved coloring each box, and suddenly, his feelings didn't seem so messy anymore - they had names and colors.

"When you are red," said Ms. Lee, "you can try deep breaths, squeeze a ball, or tell someone how you feel. You can even draw your feelings or imagine a safe place in your mind." Winston thought about his cozy bed, his favorite stuffed animal, and felt a tiny spark of calm.

Winston started using his new tools whenever he felt nervous about switching homes or doing school activities. Even when the feelings were strong, he remembered the glitter jar, the stress ball, and slow breaths. Little by little, he realized he could handle the storm inside him.

One Friday, Winston told his parents, "I like both homes, sometimes my feelings are like a big storm inside me." His parents listened closely, surprised at how well he could explain his feelings. It felt good for Winston to be understood.

Mom and Dad talked with Ms. Rivera about ways to support Winston at home. They learned to check in, give him time to express feelings, and use his calm tools with him. It felt like everyone was on the same team now.

Together, they made a plan. Each week, Winston would share what worried him before switching homes. Mom and Dad promised to listen, offer comfort, and celebrate his courage. Winston felt proud he had a plan to help himself.

He also made a calm box with favorite toys, a cozy blanket, and a notebook for drawing feelings. Whenever he felt nervous or sad, he could open the box and feel a little safer. His calm box became his personal superhero kit.

The first few weeks were still tricky. Some days felt stormy, but Winston remembered his breathing, chart, and calm box. On tough days, he practiced extra deep breaths, and on better days, he celebrated small victories like finishing homework or talking about feelings.

Slowly, Winston noticed something wonderful: even when things changed, he could find his calm. It wasn't magic, it was practice, patience, and asking for help when he needed it. Each time he tried, the storm inside him got smaller.

He shared his feelings with Ms. Lee and Ms. Rivera, who reminded him that it was always okay to have big feelings. They praised his effort and bravery. Winston realized that feelings are not scary; they just need attention and care.

Winston realized that feelings are like waves, sometimes strong, sometimes gentle but he had tools to ride them safely. He felt proud of himself for learning to surf the waves of anxiety, love, and change.

INTRODUCTION TO FAMILIES

A Note to Families:

Life in two homes can bring both joy and challenges for children. While children may love spending time with both parents, moving back and forth between homes, adjusting to different routines, and keeping up with school and activities can sometimes feel overwhelming. These transitions can create anxiety, restlessness, and big emotions that may seem confusing—even to adults.

Winston's story is written to help children recognize that it is okay to feel anxious, worried, or sad when life changes quickly. It shows that feelings are normal, and that with gentle support and practical tools, children can learn to manage those emotions.

For parents and caregivers, this book also serves as a guide to better understand what your child is experiencing. Children often do not have the words to explain their feelings fully, and anxiety can sometimes show up as irritability, withdrawal, or frustration. By observing, listening, and offering consistent support, you help your child feel safe and understood.

Inside this book, you will see examples of strategies Winston uses to find calm:

- Practicing deep breathing
- Using a calm box filled with comforting items
- Drawing and labeling feelings
- Talking to trusted adults at school and home

These strategies not only help children manage their emotions in the moment, but also build long-term skills in self-awareness, self-regulation, and emotional resilience. This book encourages collaboration between children, parents, and educators so that children can feel supported across all environments.

Remember: big feelings are normal, and children are learning how to navigate them. With patience, understanding, and the right tools, children can face change, transitions, and uncertainty with confidence and calm.

SUPPORTING YOUR CHILD THROUGH TWO HOMES, SCHOOL, AND ACTIVITIES:

1. Listen Without Judgment:
Allow your child to share their feelings freely, without immediately offering solutions. Repeat back what they say: "It sounds like you're worried about going to Dad's house today."

2. Keep Routines Consistent:
Simple routines like breakfast, bedtime, or backpack preparation help children know what to expect and reduce anxiety. Share routines with both households.

3. Provide Tools for Calming and Coping:
- Deep breathing exercises
- Calm box with favorite toys or sensory items
- Drawing or journaling feelings
- Stress balls or fidget tools
- Visual charts to track feelings

4. Talk About Transitions Ahead of Time:
Ask your child how they feel and plan short rituals during transitions to provide reassurance.

5. Collaborate With Teachers and Therapists:
Consistency across school and home supports security and confidence.

6. Celebrate Progress, Not Perfection:
Every small step—sharing feelings, using calming strategies, completing a task—is worth praise.
-

7.   Practice Patience and Empathy:
Transitions can continue to feel challenging. Reassure your child that ups and downs are normal.

8.   Encourage Reflection and Expression:
Talking or writing about experiences from each home encourages self-awareness and control over feelings.

9.   Normalize Emotions:
Let your child know that everyone experiences worry or sadness sometimes. Modeling calm behavior reinforces these lessons.

These strategies not only help children manage their emotions in the moment, but also build long-term skills in self-awareness, self-regulation, and emotional resilience. This book encourages collaboration between children, parents, and educators so that children can feel supported across all environments.

Remember: big feelings are normal, and children are learning how to navigate them. With patience, understanding, and the right tools, children can face change, transitions, and uncertainty with confidence and calm.

WINSTON FINDS HIS CALM

Winston's First Day of Kindergarten is a heartwarming story about a young boy navigating a big transition-starting school for the very first time. Winston feels excited but also a little nervous, especially because his life looks different from other kids'. His parents are divorced, and he lives in two loving homes. As Winston walks into his new classroom, he carries the comfort of

two hugs and two kisses from both Mommy and Daddy-his special reminder that no matter where he is, he is deeply loved.

Through gentle storytelling and reassuring illustrations, this book helps young children. process back-to-school jitters, explore feelings around family changes, and embrace new beginnings with courage and love.